Poetry in action

All bridges

As the sunlight shines brightly on us
It will give us strength to really grow
The natural way of life is tremendous
Knowing we can create our portfolio

All bridges that make you cross over
From hardship to your real destiny
Can be shared, so others can turn over
To a life of full belief and certainty

The water that sustain us with life
Is a universal gift for every being?
Doesn't hurt to think of the wildlife
Our lifeline we should be overseeing

The vital trees give oxygen for everyone
Whereas the rock is truly, our foundation

Poetry by Bill Burton

Copyright © 2012 by Bill M Burton

Burton, Bill M. 1959 -
Title: **Poetry in action**

Published by Burton Publishing

Poems
ISBN 978-0-9918404-0-3

All rights reserved. No part of this publication may be reproduced or transmitted, in any form or by any means, without the prior written consent of the publisher.

Edited by Debbie L Burton

Cover designed by
digimaxcreative.com

Burton Publishing
111 St. Lucie Drive,
North York Ontario,
Canada, M9M 1T4

billburton@rogers.com

PREFACE 15

FOREWORD 16

INSPIRATION 17

    Don't wait too long 18

    Sharing 19

    Keep Your Focus..............................20

    If we are free 21

    Mental Poison...................................22

    Won't Feel Sorry 23

    Enchained..24

    Seed of encouragement 25

    Break free 26

    Faith...27

    Flame alive 28

    Struggle 29

    The Recompense 30

    Worn out..31

    New Route..32

    Merry-go-round...............................33

    Sense of urge 34

Some of us 35

Everyday task 36

You're own pace 37

Vision 38

Taking Orders 39

Nature of life 40

To Strive 41

Perfect 42

Self Challenge 43

Monday 44

Persistent 45

Be determined 46

Chained Mentally 47

From my heart 48

Time is money 49

Never give up 50

Lifetime Task 51

To Persevere 52

To Succeed 53

Noise 54

Tomorrow 55

Talking To Myself.............................56

Why Waste Time................................57

Focus 58

No one 59

Dig a little deeper 60

Conceited Habits 61

No middle ground..............................62

Virtuous Patience 63

What Time is it?................................64

NATURE..................................65

God bless our farmers 66

At the river's edge............................67

Golden Sunset 68

Ballard's Valley.................................69

Linstead City 70

It's a loon..71

Rise from my bed 72

Gift of energy 73

Angel...74

Star apple..75

Jamaican dish 76

Try-All-Top-Hill 76

Trethewey Park 77

Birds of September...........................78

Motherland 79

Thinner 80

Rapid beat...81

Long Ago Friends.............................82

Scarlet...83

Inner peace 84

LIFE STRUGGLES 85

Young Life 86

Finding 87

Groom beyond belief.......................88

Bullies 89

The Passionate Eye..........................90

Lose his crown 91

The future...92

Weakness of a Gun..........................93

Honesty...94

Compassion 95

How can..96

LOVE 97

    Love's the master 98

    Save Your Tears 99

    The tears 100

    Mystical Woman 101

    Lonesome 102

    Got to have love 103

    Is it love or lust? 104

    Soul Mate 105

    Don't waste our love 106

    Little jubbie 107

    Nubian Princesses 108

    Lonely tear.......................................109

GREED 111

- Hatred and Greed 112
- How about ours 113
- Two-Tier System 114
- Commercial living 115
- Greedy down pressers 116
- Our eyes 117
- So nice 118
- Suffering 119
- Don't cry 120
- High-tech cheaters 121
- Jealousy 122
- Ungratefulness 123
- Greediness 124
- The working class 125
- Double standard 126
- Unjust Takers 127
- The Protest Continues 128
- Reminder of death 129
- Smog in the Factory 130
- Lots of money 131

No more..132

Full time snitchers 133

Everyday snitchers 134

Self-destructive snitchers 135

Workplace atrocities.......................136

Factorization..................................137

Suit people.....................................138

The negative "n" word 139

Tears of sorrow..............................140

PERSONAL POEMS 141

    Punctuality...........................142

    Dented..................................143

    Our Twins Birthday.............144

    True Being..........................145

    Dedicational birthday 146

    Princess Ashley....................147

    From your family....................148

    Our Twins Birthday.............149

    Brisk and free 150

    As Friends 151

    Friendship......................152

    The quest for liberty 153

    Our true Destiny 154

    African Rose...................155

    Just wondering.................156

    Wholesome......................157

    Compassion 158

    True Scholar......................159

    Determined 160

    Slow and steady....................161

True inspiration 162

Opals of our heart 163

Open-mindedness 164

Humanity 165

Primrose 166

ETERNITY...............................166

    The passing of time 167

    Angela Brown 168

    Natural blend..................................169

    Tears 170

    Our gentle giant..............................171

    Gordon of love 172

    Struggles together...........................173

    Clifton Newell 174

    Chocolate Hole...............................175

    For Spitley B 176

    Florida Gal......................................177

Preface

My main objective in life is to inspire those
Who are searching for a better way of living?
These poems have a foundation of their own;
They are intended to lift you up when almost
Everything seems to be going wrong. These
Poems were written from actual experiences
And what I have observed from my
Surroundings, I would like to thank my teachers
DeLou Maureen Powell and B.B
Bent of the Junction Junior secondary school
In St, Elizabeth Jamaica W.I for believing in
Me so many years ago, my sister and editor
Debbie L Burton, my son Davey C Burton
For his website and computer genius,
Christopher Thomas, Micah Clarke, my
Family and Friends. I would like to salute all
The uplifting poets of today and those who
Have gone before me. It's truly difficult
Holding down a nine to five job and writing at
The same time. To write with clearness and
Understanding our minds and heart must be
Rested. These poems are written for the like-
Minded who wish to try a freshness of doing
Instead of giving into the struggles of life.
Poetry can give us strength to carry on when
Unwanted worries lingers. It brightens our life
When we need that extra push in the right
Direction. (The key to everlasting happiness,
Is to give love freely to all human beings)

Bill M Burton

Foreword

In this life we all have duties to carry out as
Survivors, responsibilities that have never
Been taught to us by any school or institution.
I'm fully convinced that Bill is one out of
Many who have something of substance to
Deliver into this world, in a divine order
That's coming from our creator. I've known
Bill for the past year and during my
Acquaintance with him, I notice that at no
Time was he afraid to express his views and
Opinion for the oppress conditions of the
Oppressed. Most of his life he has personally
Experienced the condition which people of
African descent has had to encounter. This
Has played a great role in our development.
Bill has carefully examined the effect that
These conditions have on our people which
Created such a dim future. He wants to
Change this way of life for the betterment of
His people through his inspired messages. I
Believe this book will deliver a clear message
That will draw us closer to examine and
Reassess our selves. Bill knows if this cycle of
Life that has been forced upon our people
Continues, it will destroy the human race.

Micah Clarke

Inspiration

Don't wait too long

Don't wait too long to get going
It's time to do what we're doing

Whenever you receive the get up and go
Take action before the light turns to low

Have sat down and let the world go by
Now our basic needs will be deny

It's not too late to stake our claim
Even though our will is almost drain

We'll have to work harder to rebuild
That doesn't mean dreams can't be fulfilled

Sharing

Sharing is the only bridge for caring
And caring has a true base in sharing

Haven't we stumbled long enough?
Time to help each other out of the rough

Strength we can muster from our sorrow
As long as we pay attention to the horror

Leading by examples is most competent
It shows how we can be really proficient

Keep Your Focus

When distraction intensifies, keep your focus. When it seems that all solution runs out, still keep your focus. When you're at the edge of giving up, that's when factual wisdom will explode.

If we are free

If we are free, why do they constantly harm us? We'll try to find a job and before they're through glancing at our resumes, they'll tell us we're not really qualified. This system is designed to keep us down, and now we'll have to break ourselves free. We'll have to create our own destiny, cause that's the only cure for this disease. This stigma of we don't know what to do, must be expose from their dreadful "bluff"

Mental Poison

Mental poison is the choice of weapon now-a- days, if we take a short nap; we might be awaken by a mental smack. Whatever we are about to undertake, be on your guard for persuading crooks.

Won't Feel Sorry

Won't feel sorry when I leave this dead- end
Labor of grind, because my goal is waiting to
Be achieved. The air I breathe will be much
Sweeter, no longer surrounded by evilness;
life will be more fulfilling.

Scrooges with faces of greed, saturate the
entire place. I can see the blood they crave
slowly dripping down their insatiable faces.

My strength had stop to rest once too often,
and now awaken by man's self-indulgence; I
Must push on through before it causes more
suffering.

Enchained

Clear to see we have enchained our mind,
body and soul as this crushing work has
taken its toll. To find our right place in life, a
balance with true living we'll have to initiate.

Seed of encouragement

We Africans are the only race, who's in a massive stagger. Because robbers had tried to destroy our history, we haven't the drive to reclaim our way of life. Today everything is inactive; our whole life is nothing but a struggle. In order to reinforce the essence of freedom, we must begin to read again.
Slavery has interrupted the human race, which pierce the heart like a spiteful dagger. We got to escape from this hurtful game, Then share the essential encouragement with our children. At this moment if we are too weak, true guidance we got to find. Shouldn't wait on chance to fix our problem, it's time to steer our existence in the right direction.

Break free

Today it's time to break free
From misguided suggestion
Time to reclaim our dignity
Finding a workable solution

No one care for us but us
Careful of much falsehood
Pretending to be glamorous
Patrolling the neighborhood

They have a pleasing trait
Waiting to shift into gear
Unworkable mental state
That will bring us despair

Now I have gotten a real break
This time I'll make no mistake

Faith

Keep the faith in what you do,
Or you will be put in a curfew.
Time is really of the essence,
As our goals is in the presence.
You can accomplish your desire,
Remember you've got to perspire.

Flame alive

To us, Garvey brought the fire within,
Paving the road that means everything.

Now we must keep the flames alive,
In spite of how difficult it is to strive.

Big boulders may stand in our way,
But we can push them out the way.

The only tool we need is to believe,
It carries out action we'll conceive.

Can feel goose bumps in my nerve,
Knowing what my goals can serve.

Struggle

Bills we'll have to tackle
As our brain start to crackle

Remember you are not alone
Everyone's crush to the bone

Even though things are tight
Search not for an idle flight

Resist the murky downbeat
And persist with the upbeat

The Recompense

Yesterday I didn't have a clue,
Today I don't know what to do.
Years have come and gone,
Still wonder what's going on.
Taking myself off the fence,
Now seeing the recompense.

Worn out

Our joints sound like they need lubricating, and our pocket books all worn out. There will always be the takers desire, at the expense of those who do the work. Let's find a new avenue, before our strength is totally wasted.

New Route

For us, time's truly running out,
Now we'll have to travel a new route.
Each time that we're making headway,
These illusive thoughts get in the way.
After we have studied and understand,
It's time to follow through with a plan.

Merry-go-round

What is it that's holding me down?
In reality, I just can't move around.

What is it that's holding me back?
In my existence, I'm way off track.

Must depart from this merry-go-round,
Or my whole survival will run aground.

Sense of urge

When receiving a sense of urge,
Our laziness must be purged.
As we build our fire stronger,
Our efforts will truly surrender.

Some of us

Some of us love being second best,
Truth is we don't want to face the test.

We all will start out oh so very strong,
Then lose sight of where we belong.

The more we are around uselessness,
It directs our energy into total distress.

Slaying real devotions in what we do,
Before our aim in life can come true.

Everyday task

Got to be ready to face everyday task,
Then in the sunshine you can bask.

Not wise been down over daily hinder,
Cause our sanity we shouldn't surrender.

If we really want to escape this mayhem,
We can find the solution to our problem.

Real answers don't come in one session,
It takes many tries before it can function.

You're own pace

Go at your own pace,
Cause life isn't a race.
Don't try to impress,
And get very careless.

Tempted to take short cut,
You may end up in a rut.
Taken your own direction,
You'll get true satisfaction.

Our life will be complete,
If we can see beyond defeat.
We can take other direction,
With motivating satisfaction.

Vision

A feeling of giving up comes over me,
But now is the best time to really see.

Got to recover my obtainable vision,
That I've lost through my indecision.

Taking Orders

Taking orders from others we'll embrace it,
being self-reliant we'll turn our backs on it.
We want to enjoy the fruit, but we're too lazy to
instigate our own initiatives. We'll trade
our birthright, for any would be promises,
while the recipients flaunt their weight
around. We can be the brains behind the
world trend, yet we don't want to transcend.

Nature of life

Through the nature of life,
Hardship will cut like a knife
We'll give our all,
But still we'll fall.
A quiet voice will speak,
To guide us when we're weak.
Keep your head up high,
Then you must continue to try.

To Strive

My option had been disconnected,
It must be found and reconnected.

No matter how hard it is to strive,
My will to do must be kept alive.

Sometimes I've felt truly beaten,
But it's only a bit of retreating.

Tomorrow will bring a new day,
And my drive to strive must obey.

Perfect

Why waste time trying to be perfect, grab a hold of life, follow through, and then reflect. Now that we've shared the compass of true inspiration, isn't it time you deal with the situation. Life's too short, for you to be completely smart, if only you will make a brand new start.

Self Challenge

Life is a challenge, taking the easy way out; you should never indulge in. When doubt had sneak in from the back door, don't go easy on the culprit, cause it's not your friend, it only want to wear you out. In your quest for passionate living, storms of hindrance always close at hand. Don't give into this negative traitor, remember your dreams, and you'll succeed.

Monday

Monday and I'm back in here again,
With machines they don't maintain.

Tried to justify why I'm still here,
Knowing these bosses don't care.

However I'm sensing a new urge,
That my laziness should be purge.

The time has come to leave this place,
Then plant a seed that I can embrace.

Persistent

When we utilize persistence,
We'll surely go the distance.

It's so easy to walk away,
But go forth without delay.

Those who tried to cut you down,
In time will vanish underground

Short cuts will destroy your luck,
Then leave you permanently stuck.

Persist though your patience is thin,
Cause sitting down you will never win.

Victory for some will take a long time,
That doesn't mean their goal isn't in-line.

Be determined

If we want to cross the road from poverty to richness, we must be determined. When it seems the whole world has turned its back on you, you must be determined.

When there is no other technique left to try, we must still be determined. Determination is the only medication, which we can use in any situation.

Chained Mentally

Sometimes we're chained mentally to a Factory, thinking it is satisfactory. But it's not too late, to leave that hurting place, even if you have to do it in many a phase.

Survival is now getting worse, and dishonesty is in automatic speed. The need to want it all is soaring, as the life of the less fortunate gets deploring. No one listens to the cry of the working people, cause they are controlled by well- paid lawyers.

Sadly we are chained mentally, to a never-ending lightless alley. Isn't it time we take a glance and see how deep we're sinking? How much tougher can life get? It's time to acquire a bona fide action
Without apology.

From my heart

As these poems flow from my heart,
They are designed to give us a new start.
Whatever gender, race, color or creed,
We should help whoever is in need.
Embracing selfishness is not unique,
Let greed stumble with its technique.

Time is money

Really, we all know that time is money
Why then do we wait for life to get sunny?
It's true; time doesn't wait for anyone
So isn't it time we all try to understand
Playing with time is such a big mistake
It kills our drive in what we undertake

Never give up

Never give up the fight,
For whatever is right.
Though living is tough,
We'll get out of the rough.

Lifetime Task

If you want to start a lifetime task,
Why stick with who only want to ask.
Never mind breathing weary doers,
Keep your focus on the can do areas.
Delay will make you nosedive,
But your dream must be kept alive
So-call friends will pretend to care,
Knowing this will prevent despair.
Stay close to the conscious light,
Then everything will be just bright.

To Persevere

When life isn't clear,
I've got to persevere.
Sticking with the puzzle,
All I have to do is hustle.

To Succeed

In order to really succeed,
We'll have to plant a fertile seed.
Feeding our brain with the right attitude,
Idleness will never try to deceive or intrude.

Noise

Lots of noise and no substance,
Only action can bring abundance.

Tomorrow

When nothing seems to be going right,
Tomorrow will bring a brand new light.

Talking To Myself

Yes I'm talking to myself,
With ideas about my wealth

For years I have tried,
Yet success won't abide.

Time to change my view,
On the things I'll pursue.

Why Waste Time

Let's not worship senseless vanity,
Then pretend we love humanity.
Why waste time with that pretence,
When all we need is common sense.

Focus

The more I try is the more I learn
Got to keep my focus and succeed
Whatever is lasting must be earned
Giving your all you'll take the lead

Countless hours at your devotion
Nothing will ever get in the way
There will always be real solution
Smart work can show us the way

I can't afford to waste one minute
And watch my dream go to sleep
Have to spend precious time in it
Then my inspiration I'll truly keep

Today all the pieces have truly link
With the needed trimmings in sync

No one

No one can keep you down,
When your plans are sound.
Don't wait for a special sign,
To start your quest on time.
Placing your goals in sight,
Finally, it will come to light.

Dig a little deeper

Dig a little deeper, being on the edge our dreams won't mature. Don't be discouraged when all doors seem closed, cause hardship will crumble in the face of perseverance. Yes times are tough, everything is in the rough, but don't lose sight of the will to do. Dig a little deeper, even when times get harder. The prize will be yours if you maintain the meticulous tasks. Many loafers will criticize, cause they are dozing with laziness. When doors are made of steel, turn up the torch much higher and melt away the mountain of hesitation. Remember when success is close at hand, frustration always have a devious plan.

Conceited Habits

Be real and shed your conceited habits, we can still make it if we really try. All the good stuff we talk about will come about, if you are willing to join the Endeavour. No one can create success alone, doesn't matter how hard they try. Self-discipline will push us in the right direction, if we can spare the time to put into practice our desires.

No middle ground

No middle ground if we really want self-liberation. Let's not encourage our lazy habits that will only bring us more uncertainty. Now what are we doing to demand respect from others? It is mighty fine to be people of color; it's time to love our self despite the brain wash influence of dividers. Clearly, we can find the strength today to pursue our providence tomorrow.

Virtuous Patience

Patience is a true virtue, which must be cared for, or soon you'll lose it forever.
If we do not get what we want right away, True patience should be given a chance. When we cannot face tomorrow, the substance of patience will come to our rescue. When the night is still and no one is around to comfort you, remember to have patience in whatever you do. When we're confused and depression won't let go, it's time to reach deeper within our most inner strength. As we are trying to find our self, give patience a chance, and for sure you'll be invited to the celebration.

What Time is it?

What time is it? It's time to know ourselves,
or they will make us into clay-like dolls and
put us on a permanent shelve.

Nature

God bless our farmers

God bless our farmers, without them, we
Would all die from starvation?
Other professions looked upon as greatness,
And what our farmers receive are big fat zeros.
It's time we show our appreciation to all the farmers
Of the universe, they are not asking for much,
Just to be acknowledged for their
Contributions before they return to the dust

At the river's edge

Sitting at the river's edge, the little fishes swim on the opposite side. Many birds singing different tunes, which keep my heart in tune. The sun is going down now, so it's best if I find my way home.

Golden Sunset

Another golden sunset beyond the hills, its beauty lingers way into the evening. Doesn't matter if you live in a shack or castle, this sunset brings to us joy everlasting. Without prejudice or malice a scattered ray of light dose the scenery with a kind of wholesome love, that is just for the taking, if you are living on the corridor of a spiritual nature.

Ballard's Valley

Want to go back to Ballard's Valley,
Where the view make our eyes dally.
No, this is not really a joke or folly,
A trip to Alside will make you jolly.

Linstead City

For the Linstead crew of 1978
MacArthur, Earl, Jim, Trevor and Billy

It's Friday again, we're off to the North Coast. Linstead City, the City of mist and rain. Constant showers, which brings flowers in April and June. Going up Spur Tree Hill, with several tons, the Land Rover cries for mercy. Many miles along the way, the Rover never fails us, even on a windy rainy day. It wouldn't be wise to rough up the turn at Flat Bridge; we might capsize and never be seen again. Traveling through Bog-Walk fog so thick, you can hardly see. Passing through the luscious green brings true clearness from within. Up ahead a reminder of Mother Nature on both sides of the road. Linstead city, it's so pretty, driving through transcend such beauty.

It's a loon

Can you hear that vibrant tune?
You could easily tell it's a loon.

Rise from my bed

Tried to rise from my bed this morn', but my weariness kept me in until the sunlight disappeared. Now the birds went home to sleep, their sweet music I've missed five days in a row.

Gift of energy

As the sun rises in the summer time, it
Brought sweet gift of energy to all who is in
Sight. Roses of many colors, will beautify our
surroundings with all the rejuvenating we
need, scented flowers, they bloom all day
long, then rested in the evening,
Now the sun is off to a distant land, but
tomorrow it will be back vibrant and strong.

Angel

Angel of true light guide us to do what is right. When we falter, leave us not to be in doubt. Help us to keep our thoughts in perspective, because it's so easy to be Intercepted.

Angel of true light guide us to do what is right. With all this destructive noise, teach us how to be poised. Where all races are concern, isn't it time we live in peace

Angel of true light guide us to do what is right. Please take away the fright that lingers through the darkest of night. If only we could get a hold of the light, then tomorrow we would be able to glide and have a safe flight.

Star apple

Star apple such a stingy fruit, when ripen, it
Will not share its meaty fruit. There it will
stay, till the cows come home; never will it
fall to the ground, even on a very windy day.
If you have ever tasted this star of a fruit,
purple or green, I'm sure you'll make a
scrumptious scene.

Jamaican dish

Breadfruit, dumpling, ackee and codfish,
we'll always relish, just want to go back
home to Jamaica so we can get it fresh.

Try-All -Top -Hill

Try -All St-Elizabeth the W.I where I was
born, most of the nation has so much warmth.
Jamaica as a whole, the people are so
humble, they will give you their last cup of
love. Today the seasons are changing; our
fruit trees had all been rearranged. Long ago
trees would just sit there and does nothing;
nowadays they are bearing giant fruits that
Dangled from massive stems.

Trethewey Park

Sitting on the riverbank, waiting for the birds to sing. Automobiles of many sound constantly interrupting. Tried to focus on the birds ahead, but a wise guy shouted and they flew away. The cool breeze felt so refreshing; anything else would have to retreat. Time surely had changed at Trethewey Park, now there's a clean path where we can walk. The trees and river, truly a beautiful sight, they correspond with our senses with a pleasant delight.

Birds of September

For Chang
Red dutt Jacky-hill JA

Using bamboos in Jacky-hill,
Chang lured the birds at will.
Catching them every year,
As they take a rest from the air.

Seeing these birds of September,
Is a beautiful sight to ponder?
Jacky-Hill a place to remember,
That's where the birds flew over.

Making this trip every September.
In the cool month of September
A sea of birds in the big blue sky
It's hard to ignore, even if you try.

Motherland

Motherland of the human race,
Your beauty is of such warmth and grace.

They tried to smash your beauty from within
Still your gracious love is the real thing.

The follies of the world can't compare,
All the love that you possess and share.

Mother Africa we'll always embrace,
Acknowledging her gift to the human race.

Thinner

Some of us are trying to be thinner,
Do remember you're the breadwinner.

Looking good is our universal right,
Then keep it safe in all types of light.

Rapid beat

Listen to the rapid beat of your frightened heart, don't get carried away, cause it might not restart.

Long Ago Friends

Long ago friends with bright smiling faces, brings joy to your soul, which wealth can't replace. The warmth flows deep within our heart that's why some friends will never go away. Their kindness reminds us of the good old days, days that we'll never let go.

Scarlet

While waiting on Flight 983, I met Scarlet. Moments later we discussed the philosophies of Marcus Garvey. With Scarlet by my side, life will be a magical ride.

Inner peace

Inner peace shouldn't be a difficult task; it will participate if you sincerely ask. Life is a beautiful thing when it's shared; nothing in the whole world can compare.

Life struggles

Young Life

Today it's a world-wide epidemic
People's lives are ever so cheap
The need for vanity is never-ending
Young life snuff out without hesitation
And you'll pay for your involvement
Walking around without a bit of remorse
Tomorrow you'll get up for your new day
while relatives of the young man suffers
Though you think you're mighty and strong
If you live to be old, guilt will suffocate your
existence.

Finding

To really find a calm place,
Those days have been erase.
Can't even have a quiet lunch,
Useless noises come by the bunch.

Groom beyond belief

You can call him whatever you want, so they call him whatever they want. Never mind the respect, which should be given. Doing what they want to do, our broods were auctioned off to the highest bidder. As we get older, time appear to move faster. Yes, I know most likely, they won't care for him. Especially, when groomed at such a young age. Doubt if he will ever see them again, but do you think that will ever ease the hurt

Bullies

Bullies in our schools, break the rule,
At times they can get very, very cruel.

They brought fear to their schoolmate,
As they waited after school, to permeate.

Bullies will take out their frustration,
On bystanders without provocation.

Love to hate you if you are different,
Then leave you without one red cent.

Teachers are in a difficult situation,
Worse of all it's all over the nation.

Some parents are trying to help out,
While others point fingers and shout.

Every year it's getting worse and worse
Victim's final ride is in the back of a hearse.

The Passionate Eye

Watch what you're doing, cause the passionate eye won't lie. They will root out the mystery and shed light on the catastrophe. The world at large can pretend, but the passionate eye, the truth it will defend. When you've abused the rights of others, in due time your lustrous future will become undone.

Lose his crown

Jimmy went downtown and lose his crown the cops kept on searching but it couldn't be found. Days later, an old lady was passing by, there was Jimmy's head filled up with lead hidden so innocently, with tears running down her face, she screams in a terrified rage, saying out loud why can't our young people turn over a new and loving page.

The future

There I was worrying about the future at eight years old, and hardly started to live in the present time. It's as if the whole world was on my shoulder, seeing how some people can become so very cold.

Weakness of a Gun

Don't show off your scared self with a gun,
Cause soon you'll be on a permanent run.
Much time spent on hurting each other,
Finding whatever is required to smother.
Excuse, thank you, and please, is decease,
That's why much damage is on the increase

Honesty

With honesty and trust,
Longevity is a must.
Waste not your time,
Committing useless crime.
Sitting in prison is not a joke,
Cause your liberty will be revoked.

Compassion

Why can't we have compassion, instead
we're pumping lead in our brother's head.
Why are we deliberately trying to eradicate
the human race, then speaks of liberty for
those who can hardly keep up the pace.

How can

How can tomorrow be bright?
When all we ever do is fight.
Whether morning, noon or night,
We will destroy what's in sight.
Time to take life to a higher stage,
And get rid of the unwanted rage.

LOVE

Love's the master

Love knows no color,
Yet some hearts so hollow.
We may pretend for a while,
Then realize it's out of style.
Foolish hate may linger,
But true love's the master.

Save Your Tears

Save your tears, why pretend that you really
love me. Soon I'll no longer have to worry,
cause I'll be taking the southbound train.
You don't even have to remember my name.
I'm so tired of your foolish behavior, if I
stick around, surely I'll go insane.

The tears

No need to wipe the tears, cause they're dry anyway. Stop pretending we're still in love, cause we no longer care. Don't have to call me on the phone, our time has run its course. We must go our separate ways, now that our love has been replaced. Won't try to hold on anymore, it's time to see what is real. I'm sure we'll remember a good moment here and there, but the bad times won't be far away.

Mystical Woman

A spiritual woman I've found, she just wants to make me dance. Her mystical smile is one of a kind that I will treasure for a lifetime. She speaks of honesty, now I will be a true optimist. Her charm awakes me late at night, then I'll have to kiss her precise. Lips so tender and satisfying, they tend to agree with my motive. Mystical woman, take my heart, so we'll never be at a distance. Today I've found someone whom I believed to be profound. Her charm awakes me late at night, then I'll have to kiss her precise.

Lonesome

I'm here thinking life would be nicer,
If my lover were just a little bit closer.
Pretending that she really, really care
All I've got is a pretentious love affair
Weeks and years have gone on by,
But here I've remained a lonesome guy.

Got to have love

We've got to have love, before we can give it. We've got to share love, before we can enjoy it. We've got to dare to love, before we can claim it. Love, true love, knows no boundaries.

Is it love or lust?

She tried to get my attention, but is it love or lust. Her beauty melts my most inner being; and her perfume gives a splash of forget me not. Can't get carried away, because some would- be love never stayed. I'll try not to show that I'm anxious; don't want to give her the wrong impression. I've got to wait and see if she's for real, is it love or lust.

Soul Mate

Who will pick you up when you're down?
It takes so much energy just to get around.
If there's no soul mate to raise you up again
your confidence might endure a lot of strain.

Don't waste our love

Don't waste our love with foolish game,
because our life would never be the same.

Won't need approval if this or that say,
Those friends we've got to keep at bay.

To be different, they think we're foolish,
But we won't sit down and live sluggish.

We've got to move forward right now
Applying our energy where times allow.

Can't have negative people around us
Whose ambition is to constantly fuss?

Living free of tangled debris is essential,
It will give us strength, which is crucial

Little jubbie

Met a little jubbie from out a lane,
Suddenly my heart finds its aim.
Now I've really got to confess,
Her beauty put my nerve to the test.
I know I shouldn't get carried away,
But her smile leads my heart astray.
You might say that I was a bit weak,
But this little jubbie was very unique.

Nubian Princesses

Free up our Nubian princesses, don't you ever keep them in misery? Our African Women we must learn to protect, why then are you exchanging diamond and pearls for our African Queens. Have you all lost your imprudent minds?

Lonely tear

Shed not your lonely tear, cause now we're apart, maybe what we both need is a fresh start. Trying to find the perfect girl is a Labor of love, cause some people wear a hidden mask. Guess I'll keep on living without my angel of a bride, this tidal wave I'll continue to ride.

Greed

Hatred and Greed

Hatred and greed, always breeds a multitude
of infected seeds. There you are, talking
about good deed, but your scrupulous deeds,
always hurt someone in need.

You say I know where this is going to lead,
 and then you bleed the will of the people and
destroy their thirsty trees. These fools
Seemed intrigued by your coldness of
brutality, because you had dissected their
self-determination unfortunately.

So many eyes have been covered with
laziness, and now the whole damn world is in
a major crisis.

How about ours

How about "Us" instead of "I," How about
"We" instead of "My." How about ours
instead of yours. We need to guide ourselves
out of these chains of going nowhere
with selfishness. I'm not Mr. knows this or that,
that kind of urge would have to be cleansed.
The contribution of love can cause no pain
We better start giving it now, or we all will
go down the drain.

Two-Tier System

I'm here to expose the corrupted humans, who practice a two-tier system? Thinking they are better than other people, some overloaded fools are demanding to be treated as superiors? Crippling society as a whole, they buy their way to the front of the line. With brains no bigger than a nut, they show off their elusive influence. And so, morality is vaguely mention, yet every chance they get, they share the spoils corruptively.

Commercial living

Commercial living destroying our life,
And it's so hard to handle the strife.

Some say bigger is actually better,
But who's receiving all the glitter.

The needy being robbed as we speak,
As a better life they are trying to seek.

Downsizing comes in many cute names,
Yet we know who's pocketing the gains.

Bare face crooks are the name of the game;
they are design to drive the innocent insane

Greedy down pressers

Another nightmare last night,
Nothing seems to be going right.
These outrageous bills out of control,
In the end, they might just take its toll.
Tried to put a bit away for rainy day,
But inflation eats most of it away.
Purchasing power dwindling as we speak,
We haven't gotten a raise and it looks bleak.
Greedy down pressers pretending they care,
Treating us unfairly with no change to spare.

Our eyes

When our eyes are covered with what we should have or what we've acquired a life of insomnia we'll learn to regret. Life isn't all about wanting everything we see; sometimes it's about giving generously. Much happiness has been wasted, thinking of the world's ego, only to realize the mistake they've made.

So nice

We are so nice, protecting the people who deceived us. Trying to buy friendship at any cost, and deliberately forgetting that they are traitors of life. The future has us in the dark, now a long road we'll have to travel. The present times we think is good, but look around and you can see our existence is really convoluted. So we have a good job, then our great fortitude they will steal. We are so nice, we've settled for second best while the hungry downsizers run away with the whole prize. We are hypnotized by the bait they put before us, not seeing the trap they have created on a slender string.

Suffering

Speaking of the people and their suffering is not a popular subject. It exposes the culprits who use them in order to enhance their own way of lofty living. They will cover up the blistered heart of the common people and then pretend this is the way it should be. As these years of pain become more unbearable, you must be tough to handle these atrocities. Economical enslavement of the have not, has driven them under ground and there they will eventually perish. Some of us give so much unwisely thinking that being some sort of a second hand banana the dominator will someday feel sorry and give us our fare share of the pie. Please don't wait to be pity, cause their appetite has no ending sight and worse of all, they think that it's all right.

Don't cry

Don't cry when your money tree withered and
die. All those years we've slaved for you and
all we've got were the crumbs from the table.
Greed has mastered your only way of life,
now we can see your empire's tumbling
down. We've gotten into the cars this
morning crank up the engine as it screams
out before starting. Thirty below zero and
you've got to have the courage of a hero.
Only after we've reached the workplace, the
heater started to function just a little bit. Then
we'll work with your ungrateful way of
existence, only to pay some of our bills,
which is long overdue with added interest
in pursue.

High-tech cheaters

High tech cheaters only goal is to cheat the underprivileged. We have been cheated out of revenues and it's time for them to reinstate what's ours. We may be nervous, but remember the takers won't give it back without a fight. Sitting here writing these poems isn't hard, we only have to look around us and the evidence of our suffering is everywhere. High tech greediness trying to destroy all signs of humanity, but never mind those cruel beasts, their inhumane nature they can't escape.

Jealousy

Jealousy arise in a distracted mind,
And lasting peace you'll never find.
Don't desire the fruit of another,
It's time to find your own endeavour.

Ungratefulness

Ungratefulness is your greatest passion
Scorning the commitment of the masses
Who treated you with true compassion?
More and more you're promises clashes

Cause greed is your only objective
Ignoring the hardship that is around
Giving perks to your very selective
Then expect us to treat you profound

From now on, we'll no longer pretend
That you are really a caring person
Making sure your control is apprehend
Now that you're dictating have worsen

We'll expose your lies from the start
And from society you'll slowly depart

Greediness

The harder we really work,
The more greediness smirk.

Hiding in suspicious places,
Bosses with conceited faces.

We are so weary and tired,
Soon we won't be for hired.

The working class

Downsizing is the name of the game,
Which leaves most workers in pain?
Workplace principles is now dead,
The working people can't get ahead.

Double standard

Double standard is destroying the Holy Grail of humanity, which is certain to shorten life's expectancy. Today we're crying for peace, yet tomorrow we are as greedy as yesterday. We've disregarded the cause of universal distress, with our hearts open to self-centeredness.

Unjust Takers

Life could be better if they would stop digging into our purses. We don't have money to spend. But greedy lawmakers think we are their takers. Seems we can't get away from these heartless beasts. They have no conscience, and very proud of their feast. Doesn't matter if your car is old or new, all governments are designed to ticket you.

The Protest Continues

The protest continues working harder, and being paid lesser. Can't keep up with the hidden taxes, it just make our foundation collapses. Government playing tricks as more workers struggles, morality is lost in the ditch, and it must be found so it can be stitch.

Reminder of death

The reminder of death drips slowly from that
big oak tree. They'd hang the whole family,
one cold and bloody night. Though they
struggled for the right for liberty and life,
they still execute the helpless worn out souls.
The love for riches has be-clouded the human
race, now a great promise of contribution
is at a total lost. Today as the world pretends
everything is running smooth, the blood is
still dripping from that big oak tree.

Smog in the Factory

It's July third, and the heat is unbearable in the factory where we work. The temperature makes some worker's go off their rocker, With no recourse to take. Ventilation is nowhere to be found, as the owners are too cheap, they expect us to work and don't make a sound.

Lots of money

When you've got lots of money, everybody wants to be your best friend. As soon as the money is done, they'll leave one by one. Playing tricks is a national past time; most people want what's really yours and mine.

No more

Won't cry no more when they try to persecute the truth, cause truth has the power that no one can demolish. When my days get longer and nights are colder won't cry any more. When I'm down on my luck, still I will cry no more. Life will always deliver, when you've put in the work, the answers you seek is never far away when you refuse to give in.

Full time snitchers

They will snitch till their heart's content. In the work place, grown human snitching away the last bit of sanity they now have then tomorrow our children's, children will still be in distress. Making the rich, richer.

These full time snitchers someday hope and pray that they will be secured, but the only thing they will receive is a bucket of shaving cream. They are trying to live a life of significance, at the expense of others.

These snitchers shouting out for freedom, but for them that day will never come. They will die within the walls of betrayal, which they have set up for their foolish protection. Nothing can save the traitors of emptiness that preyed upon the existence of honesty.

Everyday snitchers

Everyday snitchers living a life of make-belief, trying to snitch their way to a big promotion. A sense of security occupied their fruitless selves, and sadly, they will introduce it to the children of tomorrow.

Self-destructive snitchers

Days had gone by, months has gone by, years has gone by, centuries are a thing of the past, and for the working class the world stand still. Self-destructive snitchers are ever so blind, their eyes are covered by arrogance and we'll now have to let them be.

I'm sure the key to our success won't be lead by these snitchers, they have peep through any little cubbyhole they can find only to inform on the working people. Why is it so hard to understand that whenever we snitch, we'll also feel the sharp edge of the push?

Workplace atrocities

While most of us pretending that life's okay, our way of living has steadily decayed. Workplace atrocities mounting higher than Everest, as hungry beast is in for the big kill. Some workers treated like second hand tools then made to look like pointless fools. Promotions for the deprived will have to work twice as hard, and still they won't receive a fare wage. Isn't it time we cut out the root of our downfall, then look at the cause of the problem? Waste not your time destroying another, that's not the solution to your global quest. The only benefactors of this obstruction are the suppressers and that's a horrible way to live. They may try to enjoy the blood of others, but soon time will catch up to them. We must cut each other's throats just to pay the rent, and yet they are not satisfied. A worker who has not the inclination of their strength from within, searching for liberty they just don't know where to begin. Freedom seekers just remember if you seek a little bit longer in a different place, you will find your true vocation.

Factorization

When one's brain is factorized, it's totally hypnotized and very difficult to refresh. Devoting your livelihood to the factory, cuts off any chance of achievement, which in time we'll learn to resent. A quick paycheck is enticing, but those trees won't bear the best fruit. To free up our brains, we must open our minds to new insights from within ourselves. Only suggesting we should take the necessary chances to become what we really want to be. It's time we are awake from this lifeless slumber. We will neglect our own dreams and build other people's reality. Now you have received the sustenance to plant you're thirsty seed, make the most of the time you've got in every way that you can ever imagine.

Suit people

Hard working men and woman do exist, the world does not comprise of suit people only. Today society has ignored and labeled all the hard working people of the world. As these lines are written, strategies are being implemented how to keep the unfortunates behind closed doors. Today we only heard of the pencil pushers as if they are the one who's providing the essential food, clothing and shelter, isn't it time, we all recognize the genuine providers of the universe.

The negative "n" word

What is it with this negative "n" word? We have it for coffee, breakfast, lunch, dinner and snacks then we demand respect from other nations. The airway is stifled with it, some of us embrace it, even making loads of money and pretending that it's the in ting. Remember what happen when we sit and try to arise at the same time. Now we'll have to expose these hypocrites who want to have it both ways. It's time to educate ourselves, before we are totally removed from the face of the earth. For years, self-respect has been under house arrest and hardly anyone really notice.

Tears of sorrow

When tears of sorrow surrounds you, fear not of your lonesome heart. The painful burden of the tragedy will pass, and then the sun will rise with its vital warmth. We're all faced with unexpected worrisome task, but real answers will draw closer and ease the hurt.

Personal poems

Punctuality

For all honest seekers.

Punctuality will get mix reviews, so much excuses and stores they'll make you blue. Punctuality is good medicine when taken at the right time, and then early you must go to bed so wherever you are going you'll reach on time. I've got a few friends who aren't so punctual, but with some persuasion they now agree that it's a good transformation. There are a lot of good benefits from being punctual, for one thing we don't have to rush and then cause uncertain arrival. I do believe being punctual is the tool of survival; it gives strength to those who grasp it with good intention. Punctual people always stick together; any storm they can surely weather. Excuses for me I must refuse, because punctuality can serve as our own betterment All you late comers and doers wipe the slate clean then your life will be almost complete. What you now deny, could be your passage to true freedom?

Dented
Burton sonnet

Love is of splendor when trust is guarantee
When there is no surprises waiting for you
Giving completely, we will never disagree
That we should be loyal in whatever we do

Regardless of the bait that they've presented
Years of friendship should never be dented
Today you looked really content and engage
With laughter loudly, as if you're on a stage

Whatever that will endure must be genuine
Deceits have no place in harmonious living
As we try to put food on the table and shine
Why forsaken your defender with misgiving

We shouldn't chase after an elusive alliance
When we can see a red flag with its defiance

Our Twins Birthday

For Debbie B.

Birthdays are a beautiful celebration, it furnish a brighter situation. We'll have laughter and songs of passion, singing loudly without confusion. Sharing real gift of joy, life is a precious gem that sparkles even in the dark. A mother of love, by your children you are dearly loved. Forthright you are with your ambition; you go right ahead without indecision. Happy birthday Debbie and have fun, remember we'll love you always.

True Being

For Novlyn B.

Novlyn, your kind heart reflects who a true being is. As a giver, you shall forever be of real love. You are a true example of what the world need, planting the seed of love that we so really need. As we watch you since we were younger, you're caring ways make us much stronger. At times when we are weak we look to you for guidance, cause you're so unique .You have taught us over the years, how to be aware. To share is one of your greatest traits, and hate can never infiltrate. A Caring mother you are, your children's love is never far. You are one of a kind, always putting others first with true love in mind.

Dedicational birthday

For Michelle N.

Dedication is one of your favorite obsessions; you have made many a sacrifice to reach safely at your destination. It's clear to see the more birthdays that you celebrate; it shows your positive trait. Kindness from you is a plus; you'll even take the long way home if it meant to be just. Happy birthday Michelle with lots of love from Ainsley, Ashley, Ethan and us, a mother at heart with eternal loving trusts.

Princess Ashley

For Ashley N.

Ashley is our latest princess; she sat there
looking pretty, in her little pink dress. Her
smile makes a dull day brighter and
happiness from within can only thrive.

With two bottom tooth she looks quite astute.
Cuddling in her mother's arm, she looks at
her dad, with a true sense of love and calm.

From your family

For Cheryl B

Your kindness bloom over our family tree
Causes your love for all of us shines so
Excellently. In times of need you comfort us,
Without making any sort of fuss? A great
Mom you are who cares for your children and
Other children's of the world. A sense of
Giving is your life's work; anything less just
Wouldn't work. Your siblings do love you;
We say many thanks for all the things you do.
 Your children's love for you is in
Abundant, cause they know caring for them
You're never reluctant.

Our Twins Birthday

For Jessie B.

As we congregate for another birthday, togetherness is so heartily. Times moving expediently, seems we're having birthdays more frequently. It's good to celebrate our birthday with family and friends, it keep us together with a natural trend. Those you've inspired, have acquired their desire. Happy birthday Jessie and have fun, remember we'll love you always.

Brisk and free

For Christopher T.

Wherever we'll be, have to remain brisk and free. Won't hesitate to infiltrate all negative destructive traits. Remembering where we have to go, keeping the true inner light a glow. As time moves on, seeing what life have to offer, never losing sight that tomorrow will have the answer. Facing the struggles together, learning how hard a life we must weather. Standing firm with enduring plans, we'll find our castle that will be so grand. The truth with the guiding hand, won't be far when we need a hand. Knowing that dreams come true, we'll search for the tools to do

As Friends

For Wayne A.

As friends we've gone separate ways, but true respect will always stay. Though they have tried to dissect our friendship, our brotherly love can never face hardship. Going through life's everyday task, we'll have to keep the faith to face each and every task. New beginnings will be different; we just have to learn how to make the adjustment. Respect you have demanded from everyone, that's why our friendship will always have the upper hand.

Friendship

For Clifton M.

Friendship is the foundation, the foundation
of any honest situation. Through the years
we've face many rough seas, but we
reminded each other of the calm sea to be.
Facing the struggles of today and tomorrow,
life can be overwhelming with our sorrows.
Remembering those who's worse off, we
gladly appreciate what we now enjoy. Years
have rolled beyond our wildest dream, yet
mutual respect remains the only theme.
Before us will be new challenges, face them
with persistency. With tranquility on our
side, we shall move with grace through life.
True friendship is forever; they guide us
through all endeavors

The quest for liberty

For Mica C.

The quest for liberty is your chief aim in life, though it's an uphill battle, you'll always strive. Remembering the reason for such a huge task, we'll be giving our support without been ask. For all "who" puts in the effort for the cause, we salute you with all our heart. It takes a willingness to give, and for you that's the only way to live. Interruption will show their disruptive faces, then they'll be enlighten and shown their rightful places. Self-empowerment is your destination; together we'll find the solution.

Our true Destiny

For Patrice and Jessie B.

As I am for you and you for me, let love rule our destiny. When troubled times try to obstruct our plans, we'll remember where our true hearts belong. So glad we are, that we've found each other, now we can share our love, as we desire. Cause love is what we've truly found; on anything less we'll surely frown. Where trust is concerned, time has showed it's earned. So remember now that we have god's blessing, our ponient love will live forever. Through thick and thin, sadness, joy and happiness we'll be together. Reaching out for each other was the best thing to do, so let love rule .As you for me, me for you.

African Rose

For Teresa P

An African rose you are, giving so much love to the rest of the world. Treating everyone with kindness, then you shall live free in trueness. As you love to share in your doing, then we shall wish you and your family good luck in all you're doing. With respect from us to you, we know that life's gonna treat you good in whatever you do.

Just wondering

So you didn't have the courage to say goodbye. Giving your friend the letter that put me in a daze. We use to have such a good time. A day doesn't go by, that I don't think of you. Treated me like a king, but didn't have a chance to treat you like a Queen. Sitting here just wondering how different life could have been, if you had chosen to stay. Whatever transpires in life, I will always remember you and I know you feel the same way too? Your tender loving care is never far from my mind. Where are you now? Seems my love for you will never expire.

Wholesome

For Emily and Leo B.

A wholesome lady we've known for a long time, a loving kind- hearted friend that gives her all, all the time. She treats who's around her with great respect, then her daily living it does reflect. Honesty is cherished as time goes by, could not hurt another even if she tries. Living a life of wholesomeness, bonding with Leo with blessedness. With truly blessedness

Compassion

Compassion is like a rear gem these days, most people who give just want to be paid. We've experience the nature of your giving ways, a combination of trust and care, you've share with the rest of the world. We are sure this kind of inner strength will be passing on to the next generations, with assurance that it will be of great celebration. Kindness can be the bridge for all beings, ''who'' need to cross to the other side of certainty. To start a task we should, but to finish is the ultimate dream. You are always willingly reaching out to make a difference, for that you shall receive such true grace from within.

True Scholar

For Dereck L M.

Dereck is a true scholar, the fallies of life he'll never acquire.
Standing up for what is right, he won't give up, and he'll fight.
Many a men tried to persecute him, but their chance was very slim.
So many years working together, we've weather many storms;
these memories will last forever. We've traveled on that bumpy road
for long time, but now, as we look back, it's all fine. Facing the
years to come, with clearness to see beyond. The road has been
paved for a joyful life, now go forward cause you can only strive.

Determined

For David N. R.

For you, being determined is a way of life, knocking down all kind of strife. You know what it takes to reach your goals, never embracing lazy strolls. Watching you from a distance, you are all persistence. As we defend truth and rights together, those days will always be remembered. There is a different way of life for truehearted friends, because the truth they always defend.

Slow and steady

For Bidyut K. D.

Slow and steady, soon your destiny will come. Travelling too fast could be out of control. The time has come to be conscious, conscious of which road is clear. Life experience is the teacher of time, so get back in line with your journey in mind. When we have the will to become, the world will accept our decision. Don't be afraid to take charge of any situation, even though you are surrounded by frustration. Think of winning no matter how small, cause a doing heart can never fall. The ships you've sent out forever so long will know that home is where they belong. Staying close to nature its blessedness, a life of trueness, brings forth sureness.

True inspiration

For Reggae Singer. Emissary Ras Shiloh

True inspiration is from our inner most, and then we'll let it loose where it's needed most. Sharing wisdom with the weak, so their tomorrow won't be bleak. To give is a liberating force, it guides hungry souls then they'll take the right course. An honest life is the best; there's no competition to see who is the best. Ras Shiloh an emissary at heart, a true inspirator that teaches from the heart. With uplifting messages that won't leave ever, you've given us the tools of awareness that will be with us forever.

Opals of our heart

For Gia and Christopher T.

We are the opals of each other's heart, then how could land and sea keep us apart. As we wait to repatriate, we only have to keep the faith. We'll remain in unison of true love, cause we were meant to be like a pair of inseparable doves. Struggles of our future will try to interfere; we only have to remind each other how much we really cared. As our children are the love of life, together we can only strive. Gia, you're sweeter than all the jasmine flowers of the world, Christopher, your tender love is as fresh as the mountain zest, that only true love can impress.

Open-mindedness

Open- mindedness is a sturdy bridge; it helps us to cross over all kind of disadvantage. Giving strangers the benefit of a doubt, it creates a climate of harmony that doesn't shout. When we rush to past judgment, there can be no broad scope of betterment. The world would be free of unkindness, if we could act with more tolerance and kindness. With all the different tribes in the world, if we could taste unconditional love for each other, this useless hate we wouldn't have to live under and suffer. When we can feel the pain that's been inflicted on the innocent, a more beautiful world will be in existence.

Humanity

For Dough L.

As we can see, the love of humanity is in you, because it reflects the things you say and do. At times it's hard to find people who care, but it's easy to detect that you really care. Around us are those who deceive to achieve, we'll feel sorry for them and let them be. In time we will go our separate ways, but remembering kindness we always obeyed. Some days will be tough, thinking about how life should have been, but we must dig much deeper, if we want to be seen. There is a beautiful rose on a distant hill, go now and enjoy its fragrance until you have your fill.

Primrose

For Primrose

Prim is my genuine rose; to her I can't wait to propose. Her tender heart has now bound us forever, and it's time to spend the rest of our years together. Primrose, take my heart lover of all loveliness, without your guiding light my boat would surely run a wreck. Woman of such bright taste, reaching home I've got to make haste. With a blend of love and kindness, I'll await your receptiveness. I can rely on your inner beauty; because honesty is your only duty. Prim I'm gonna fill your cup with true love, all the way up to the brim. My sweet rose, with such gentle prose. Understanding the rough cuts of life you are here for me, then I'll never dish you hearth no matter how frustrating life might be. Primrose stay close to my heart, cause in life or death we shall never part.

Eternity

The passing of time

The passing of time brought us more in line, With what is really important today. In reality we lived in a world of ups and downs, busily trying to figure out what to complete. Excitement of the world trend stretches way beyond and when death is at hand, everything seems so insignificant. Not saying for you to search for tribulation, but these are uncertainties we all have to face. Have you ever thought of getting old and helpless, it brings a chill to our mind's eye? We'll miss those who went before us, and then time will destroy our petite existence.

Angela Brown
Our Classmate

For Angela B.

Woodside District
Ballard's Valley Primary School.
South East St. Elizabeth Jamaica W.I.

The School bell rings, but she wasn't sitting
at her desk. Never had she been late before,
and then slowly Miss Neil told us, she was no
more.

Angela Brown was the kind of classmate,
which never frowned. We'll always
remember her with her little brown grip. And
losing her we'll never come to grip.

Calmness was her finest trait and that no one
can ever debate. She will always be in our
memories; we know she had a short journey
to heaven. Rest our little angel; rest in the
arms of the creator.

Natural blend
Grand Mother Rosa and her two sisters

For Rosa, Lynette and Shem

Rosa, Lynette and Shem, they were a natural blend. Three sisters that shared one common bond of love, a connection with kindness that only goodness can reflect. Across from the gully where they lived, all three homes in view of each other, they only had to gaze quietly and where help is needed it will be rendered immediately. They were true examples of how siblings should live; their main goal in life was to give. A lifetime of lesson was given, for those who seek it. Their way of life was of gentleness, leaving in their path all pure blessedness. Their contribution will be with us forever, showing us the way to prosper. A triple season of compassion was anchored in our minds and hearts, then their true living will always give us a new start, Honesty was the only way of life, and they have leaved us with a first class way to strive.

Tears
Our Cousin

For Sandra L.D.

Our tears continue to flow, when it will stop?
No one really knows .Our love for Sandra
will never end; she was a true mother, sister,
niece, cousin and friend. Every time she
comes to mind, we'll keep her kindness in
mind. The time has come to say good- bye,
but her memories we will never let go. We
have grown together as one, so how can true
love ever disband. Oh true god of mercy;
release us from this painful flight. As our
heart ache from day to day, our love for her
will never go astray. She was a caring mom,
who provides for her children the best way
she could. Now she's gone out of sight, but
will never be out of our heart and mind. Ever
much so loved. Our Sally forever.

Our gentle giant
Cousin

For Keron L B

Though you have gone before us, we will never forget your gentle kindness. Time will not erode your memory from our hearts, even though you have departed. We'll cherish the short time you have spent with us; your caring ways was tremendous. We had shed many tears of sadness, knowing that you are no longer with us. As we put revenge out of our midst, then we'll plant a flower of love within. Feeling sorry for the culprits that brought about our lost, one day they will realized the significant of our lost. Love is the master of our pain; it heals the hurt and brings forth restraint.

Gordon of love
Friend

For Ivy M.G.

Ivy Gordon, our true Gordon of love. We have no doubt that she's flying high with her two extra sets of wings, way beyond the Milky Way. Her kindness from within, have given us a bridge to cross in our times of troubles. We'll keep her Gordon of love free of hate and malice; because that's the only way we'll enjoy her Gordon of love. Whenever we stumbled, a word of encouragement is never far away, she always take the time to put us on the right track. With four wings, good tidings she'll forever bring. Our true Gordon of love, flying high like a wholesome dove. Like a wholesome dove, whom we'll forever loved.

Struggles together
Friend

For Lovilda H Smith

Twenty years of struggles together, we work under many a pressures. As we linger in each other's mind, good memories we'll truly find. When friends are in one location, yesterday is always the conversation. Things we use to frown about, with maturity, no longer come about, doesn't matter where we go; our brotherly love will also glow.

Clifton Newell
Friend

For Clifton N.

We've made a promise to Cliff, to spread the word of love and honesty. Calm and quiet he was, never making useless fuss. Emphasizing the need for peace among mankind, he dwells on the foundation of pure love. It was a pleasure to have work with him; he has opened our eyes to many uplifting things. As the sun sparkles on his words of forgiveness, we are sure he is resting in a bright light of peace. Always finding time to give, and so the goodness in him will forever lived. A teacher of kindness, he teaches by example. Now you're resting quietly beyond our reach, we'll remember that love is within our reach.

Chocolate Hole
Grand parents

For Judy and Dearest D.

Judy and her dearest love, they were like the most beautiful doves. With true giving hearts, it's so easy for them to get a fresh start in whatever they had perused. Judy was our life and protector at all cost, never mind what's the cost. A woman of a giving agenda, she would take care of whoever was in need. With a multitude of things to accomplish, they would carry out each task until it was accomplished. A true businesswoman, she was articulate in a life of adventure. As they rest quietly under the fruit trees, our heart is contented knowing they are at peace.

For Spitley B
Our Cousin

Our teacher is now resting quietly in his own space; let's learn from him how to love the human race. We'll miss Baton when we think of love; he is a true example of what the world is missing. We've cried tears of sadness day and night; our love for him will forever shine bright. Many more tears will flow, because his kindness we'll never let go. His goodness, he shared with me, that's why I see so clearly. He speaks yesterday with a loud voice strong with passion; today we'll remember his trueness without confusion. Our love will be with Eula and the children always, even though some of us are so far away.

Florida Gal

For Stanford B. and crew
Grand father

Pedro's Florida Gal, the most reliable fishing Boat of its time. It must have been tough handling the sails and ores; a fisherman job wasn't an easy chore. Walking down the steep hill of look out, it echoes when you slightly shout. Don't lose your footing, cause there will be a lot of looting. Florida Gal has been providing for the family for many years, catching fish abundantly. One dark and cloudy night the storm came and Florida Gal parted waves into pieces, many tears had been shed granddad said, now that Florida Gal is dead.

www.ingramcontent.com/pod-product-compliance
Lightning Source LLC
Chambersburg PA
CBHW060533100426
42743CB00009B/1511